AIRCRAFT

BY CHRISTOPHER PICK

CONTENTS

Dusseldorf airport, Germany. This airport, which is at the centre of Germany's main industrial region, is among the country's busiest.

INTRODUCTION

Autumn 1903: two young brothers – bicycle-manufacturers from Dayton, Ohio – travelled to the North Carolina coast. Day after day they struggled to get their flying machine airworthy. One problem followed another. Finally, all seemed to be ready. On 14th December, a first attempt at flight failed. Three days later came success. Watched by his brother Wilbur, Orville Wright took off in their *Flyer*, remained in the air for twelve seconds, and landed again. He had travelled (36.5 metres) 120 feet.

It was an apt beginning to the new century, for in this century man's ability to fly has had revolutionary consequences. Before 17th December 1903, the world was vast. A traveller might reckon on several days to cross the Atlantic. Afterwards, land and ocean shrank rapidly, and today breakfast in London can be followed by breakfast in New York.

Before 1903, the sky was a neutral zone in war. Afterwards, command of the skies was not only essential for success on the ground; many of the most decisive conflicts were settled in the air. Before, soldiers at the front had borne the weight of battle. Afterwards, the battle would suddenly come from the sky without warning to unprotected civilians.

Flight not only had revolutionary consequences; its landmarks came ever more quickly. In 1903, it was triumph enough actually to have flown. Less than six years later, Louis Blériot made the first crossing of the English Channel, and ten years later Alcock and Brown crossed the Atlantic. In June 1939 regular passenger services across the Atlantic started and in the same year came the first jet flight. In October 1947 an aircraft travelled faster than the speed of sound for the first time, in 1952 regular jet passenger services began and in 1976 supersonic ones.

Though it is to the Wright brothers that the honour of the first flight goes, the experiments of their numerous predecessors cannot be overlooked.

Man had always dreamt of flying, and birdmen feature in the folklore of many countries. Perhaps inspired by them, countless 'aviators' over the centuries equipped themselves with wings, took off from some convenient hillside, flapped their arms in vain and plunged to the ground.

The first practical steps towards flight came near the end of the eighteenth century with the introduction of the hot-air balloon. This, it is true, got men up into the air; but once there, they had no reliable means of controlling the speed of their flight or its direction. Ballooning however did inspire Sir George Cayley, an English scientist and inventor, to reflect on the problems of flight. In 1804 he built and successfully flew a model glider; five years later came a full-size glider; forty-four years after that came a third version, this one capable of carrying a passenger.

Cayley had established the principles of successful flight, and over the next half century a series of experimenters improved and refined aircraft structure. Otto Lilienthal was one of the most significant of these; certainly he can claim to be the first real aviator and had made over 2000 flights when, in 1896, he was killed when one of his gliders crashed to the ground.

All that was lacking then was some means to power an aircraft. The obvious answer was the engine of the newly invented motor car. The Wright brothers, who had already built several gliders, now attempted to adapt a car engine. The attempt failed, they designed their own, and the machine flew.

Then, on 8th August 1908, Wilbur Wright first demonstrated the Wright *Flyer A* in France. That brief moment of smooth, controlled flight electrified the European pioneers. Soon they were building far more effective aircraft, refined through the medium of racing and record attempts.

Slowly, the potential of the ever-improving machines was recognized; in 1911, mail was carried

A replica of Blériot's Type XI monoplane. On
13th July 1909 he made a cross-country flight
of 26 miles, and followed this up with his
Channel crossing.

by air for the first time, as was freight; in the same year, a Captain Piazza, a member of the Italian Expeditionary Force in North Africa, piloted the first operational military flight; in 1912, the British Royal Flying Corps was founded, and in 1914 the first scheduled airline service.

As war was declared in 1914, aircraft, though more sophisticated and reliable than the string, wood and glue machines of ten years before, were limited in their range and payload (weapons load), and thus in their uses. Military men saw them as a useful means of observing the enemy and of providing support for ground troops.

By the end of the war, four years later, a whole series of fighter planes had been developed; British planes had bombed Germany, German planes had bombed England; pitched air battles were fought, culminating in the Allied attack on the Saint-Mihiel salient when 1500 planes, from the British, American and French air forces, were thrown into battle.

In many respects – design and speed, for example – aircraft were scarcely more advanced at the end of the war than at the beginning. They were, however, at the centre of transport developments, their potential had been clearly demonstrated and commercial services started within a few months of the armistice. Regular services quickly developed between London and Paris (a $2\frac{1}{2}$-hour journey) and Paris and Brussels; and within a few years, national airlines had been established in many European countries, and most major cities were reached by some form of scheduled service.

The United States lagged behind a little. Although airmail services between New York and San Francisco had started as early as 1920, the first regular passenger flights were not inaugurated until 1925. Thereafter, the network spread rapidly. By 1927 Imperial Airways were flying from London to Pakistan; six years later they were serving India, Malaya and Australia.

A passenger in 1919 could still consider himself an adventurer. He certainly had plenty of money (the fare from London to Paris was £21); he was quite likely to be flying for the first time – and had almost certainly had to overcome his family's protests, for flying was still considered very risky (in fact, it wasn't).

His plane was made of wood; his pilot probably sat in the open; and he and his one or two fellow-passengers might have worn a coat, helmet, gloves and goggles to keep warm. His pilot took off from a grass runway, flew low and navigated by follow-ing rivers, roads and railways, helped by an ordinary map.

Nearly twenty years later, passengers still needed plenty of money. Though no longer pioneers, they were still doing something pretty unusual. Planes were probably all metal, and pilots could rely on a variety of navigational aids. The passenger's comfort was a first consideration: meals were substantial, the furnishings elegant. And the only bit of adventure he and his fellow-travellers (now rather more numerous) could expect was probably an overnight stop; if they were on a long international flight.

By the mid-1930s it had long been apparent to many military thinkers that control of the air would be essential for victory in another war. The only country that initially put this belief into practice was Germany who secretly built up and trained an airforce on Russian soil; by 1935 it had nearly 1900 planes and 20,000 men, this fact only gradually being revealed after Hitler had come to power in 1933. Britain and France responded hastily and established their own armaments programmes.

How right this belief was, was soon demonstrated. In Poland in 1939, the Luftwaffe, the German airforce, completely destroyed the Polish airforce within a few days and was then able to bomb Warsaw and harry the Polish ground forces mercilessly. As a result Poland surrendered within a month.

The story was the same as Hitler pushed westwards towards the Channel coast in May and June 1940. It was practically the same two months later as a German invasion force massed in the Channel ports of France and Belgium.

The Luftwaffe mounted an all-out assault on the airfields and radar defences of southern England but failed, though only just, to knock them out.

When peace returned, airlines took advantage of the enormous advances made during the war. Piston-engines gave way gradually to turboprop engines and then, by the late 1950s, air travel became faster and more popular: 209,000 passengers crossed the North Atlantic by air in 1947: the number was just over a million ten years later (equal, for the first time, with the number who crossed by sea), and had reached an incredible $12\frac{1}{2}$ million by 1975. In that same period, flight times between London and New York had been dramatically reduced too; from $19\frac{3}{4}$ hours in 1947 to $10\frac{1}{4}$ in 1958 and $7\frac{1}{2}$ in 1975.

The early 1970s brought another major advance,

as the supersonic English and French *Concorde* was tested and finally, amid great controversy, brought into service. Now London is within 3½ hours of New York and Bahrein, Paris within 7 hours of Rio de Janeiro.

Today, crowded airports, inflight services and safe arrivals are part of the experience of millions of people.

A replica of the *June Bug* (*below*), one of the craft designed by Glenn Curtiss, the American pioneer of water-borne aircraft. In 1908 he tried unsuccessfully to convert it into a seaplane by adding floats, renaming it the *Loon*.

A more successful water-borne aircraft (*bottom*), was the Short Sunderland, Britain's major flying boat in use during the Second World War.

7

EARLY AIRCRAFT

The history of powered flight is full of stories of individual determination and enterprise, of sudden inspiration and blind alleys. The de Havilland Hornet Moth, a wooden two-seat light plane, was used widely for primary training in the 1930s and 1940s. It was used also for military communications.

The pioneers of aviation built their own craft, almost as basic as that below, which is a modern American homebuilt. Their aim was to build an aircraft that could fly; that of today's enthusiasts is to fly as cheaply as possible. The pioneers had no knowledge of how to design efficient wings and propellers, and had no lightweight engines of high power/weight ratio. Today's homebuilder can call upon the experience of design and construction gained in more than 75 years of powered flight.

The airship (*right*) had flown long before the aeroplane. The first manned and powered airship flew in France in 1852, but 32 years passed before the first really controllable airship took to the air. Development of the airship as a passenger transport ended after the explosion of the *Hindenburg* in 1937, but vessels like this Goodyear dirigible were still flying in 1979.

The Avro Tutor (*above*), a two-seat biplane, was
used for basic pilot training. The prototype
first flew in 1930, and thereafter a considerable
number were manufactured, chiefly for military
use by both the RAF and other air forces. A few
were used in civil aviation. The Tutor had a
range of between 200 and 375 miles, and
cruised at a little over 100mph.

The Nieuport 24 (*top, opposite*) was one of the
many aircraft built for both civilian and
military use by the French Nieuport Company
during the First World War.

The Navy Curtiss NC-4 flying boat (*below,
opposite*), was the first aircraft to cross the
Atlantic. The back-up help for this project,
organized by the US Navy, was enormous. No
less than 68 Navy destroyers were stationed at
50-mile intervals across the Atlantic to assist the
three flying boats (or 'Nancy boats' as they were
nicknamed), which took off from Newfoundland
on 16th May 1919. Two failed to complete the
crossing, but NC-4 reached Lisbon on 27th May,
and Plymouth, England, four days later, after
no less than seven refuelling stops.

SMALL AIRCRAFT

Both civilian and military purchasers have found small
aircraft invaluable because of their flexibility and relative
cheapness. The two-seat Dassault-Breguet/Dornier Alpha
Jet is a light strike aircraft developed during the 1970s
by the French and Germans. Such aircraft have been made
possible by the development of small, powerful, economical
jet engines.

The de Havilland DH82 Tiger Moth (*opposite, below*), a single-engine two-seat biplane, was used by the RAF for nearly 20 years as an initial pilot-trainer. It first flew in October 1931, entering service four months later. It was highly successful, and over 1000 had been manufactured by the end of the 1930s, and a further 4000 were built during the war for the RAF, as well as nearly 3000 in New Zealand, Canada and Australia. When finally retired from the RAF Volunteer Reserve in 1951, it was the last biplane trainer still used by the service.

The experimental plane (*left*) was evolved by Bede Aircraft, an American company established to develop plans and kits of parts to assist homebuilders in the construction of light airplanes.

A ski-equipped Pilatus Porter (*top*) is seen on a glacier high in the Swiss Alps. Planes such as these are extremely useful in mountainous and remote regions, and need only a relatively small area in which to land and take off. This makes them especially suitable for mountain search and rescue tasks.

The Pitts S-1 Special sporting biplane (*opposite, top*) is a type used by many famous aerobatics teams.
Originally designed in 1943, Pitts Specials have been in production ever since, and by the mid-1970s about 300 were under construction or flying. (One version is intended for the homebuilder only.) Pilots flying Pitts Specials have achieved considerable success in aerobatic contests all over the world.

Instrument panel of a Piper Cherokee C (*above*). At first sight it seems very complex, but in its basic Standard version the four-seat Cherokee C had dual controls and only essential engine and flight instrumentation. More experienced owners could have added full blind-flying instruments, communication and navigation avionics, and a simple autopilot to maintain height and course.

The Piper PA-31-350 Navajo Chieftain (*right*) is one of the large range of light aircraft manufactured by America's Piper Aircraft Corporation. Announced in 1972, this aircraft is one of the Navajo series. Its main users are private companies who find it profitable to run their own aircraft, and commuter air services. The Chieftain is available with two different seating arrangements, the six-seat Standard and and the ten-seat Commuter. Maximum cruising speed is 254mph, and maximum loaded range over 1000 miles.

Overleaf: a fleet of light planes belonging to a New Zealand company. Small aircraft such as these, which usually seat two to eight people, are virtually air-taxis. Since all can land on grass strips, some on water, they can ferry travellers to almost anywhere. In some remote areas, such services often form the only practical means of long-distance transport.

Seaplanes

Like airships, flying boats, though successful and popular in their day, have been overtaken by modern technology. The first seaplane flew on 28th March 1910, when Henri Fabre travelled nearly one third of a mile, near Marseilles. Then initiative passed to the USA, where Glenn Curtiss developed twin floats (to give lateral stability) and added a stepped hull (to break the suction of the water when the plane took off). During the First World War, water-borne aircraft were used for both reconnaissance and attack. The inter-war years saw the development of bigger craft, the first crossing of the Atlantic (see page 13), and numerous epic long-distance flights. Prominent among these were two in 1931 by the British aviator Francis Chichester, who later became famous as a lone, round-the-world yachtsman. He made the first solo air-crossing between New Zealand and Australia in a de Havilland Gipsy Moth seaplane (rebuilding her during the journey after she had sunk). A

few weeks later he repeated the feat between Australia and Japan.

Seaplanes and flying-boats played a significant role in the Second World War, used for reconnaissance, anti-submarine patrol and rescue duties. Thereafter, the development of helicopters, and faster and larger commercial aircraft, which were able to carry out such rescue and attack duties more cheaply and in all weathers, meant that after 1945 flying-boats gradually disappeared from the mainstream of aviation.

The de Havilland DHC-3 Otter (*opposite*), developed from the de Havilland Beaver, first flew in 1951. Over 460 were built, many for the US Army and the Royal Canadian Air Force. The Otter could be equipped to operate from land, water and snow surfaces, had a range of 875 miles, and a cruising speed of 121–132mph.

The Consolidated PBY Catalina (*below*) is, like the Sunderland, one of the famous Second World War flying-boats. More than 3500 were built, of which 2000 went to the US Navy and 650 to the RAF.

A flying-boat on Lake Woahink, Oregon (*below*); and (*opposite*) two means of transport in the difficult conditions in remoter parts of Latin America: a motor boat and a seaplane. Civil uses of water-based aircraft remain numerous but specialist. They come into their own in regions such as northern Canada and Alaska, which abound with rivers and lakes. They are used for fighting forest fires in many parts of the world. In New York, they provide a daily service between Long Island and Wall Street: the ultimate in luxury commuter travel.

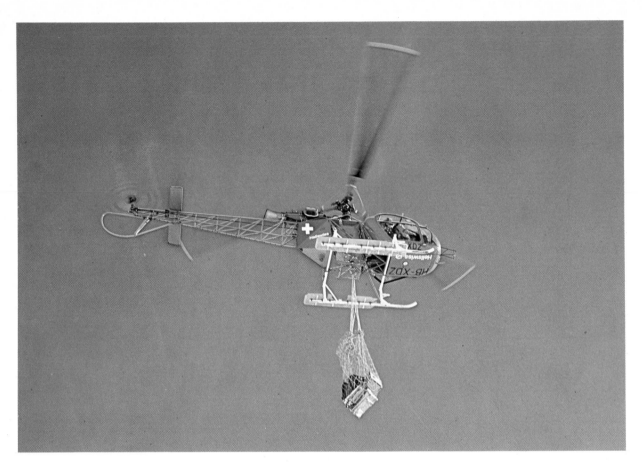

Helicopters

Helicopters such as the one illustrated on the ground and in the air (*opposite*) look very like the first examples to be used for both military and commercial operations. There is one easily recognizable feature which, however, identifies this as a modern helicopter: it is powered by a gas turbine engine, the lightweight, powerful powerplant which has revolutionized the performance of rotary-wing aircraft. It has a three-blade main rotor, which does rather more than substitute for the wings of a fixed-wing aircraft. Not only does this main rotor provide the lift necessary to raise the entire aircraft into the air, but appropriate rotor controls make it possible for the helicopter to hover at a particular height, or be flown in any direction. The small rotor at the tail, in this case of three-blade design, is known as an anti-torque rotor. Without it the entire helicopter would try to rotate in the opposite direction to the main rotor as a result of torque action.

When the lift capability of an aircraft is more important than its range and speed, basic helicopters of this kind offer considerable weight-saving by eliminating structures to enclose the complete fuselage and engine. The turbine-powered helicopter (*above*) typifies modern commercial aircraft that carry some 12–14 passengers or an equivalent load of cargo, with the capability of lifting as much as 4000–5000 pounds by means of an external cargo sling. Rotary-wing aircraft of this latter type have proved to be most important for both civil and military use, and have made a notable contribution to the development of offshore oilfields.

Gliders

Gliding is the oldest form of heavier-than-air flight. Gliders enabled the pioneers – among them Otto Lilienthal, Octave Chanute and the Wright brothers – to understand the basic principles of flight.

The essence of gliding is simple: the glider must reach flying speed, that is a speed at which its

wings generate sufficient lift to keep it airborne. Today, gliders are launched by a rope, usually about 200 feet long, attached either to a car or to another aircraft.

Although most people associate gliders with sport, many have served for aeronautical and meteorological research, and were much used in the Second World War.

A typical view (*above*) of a tug aircraft soon after take-off, with the glider still attached to the tow rope. Assisted-launch of this kind makes it possible for the glider to be released at height, or distant from its base.

The picture (*right*) emphasizes the lines of a modern high-performance sailplane. Apart from the use of advanced aerodynamic design and the high aspect-ratio wing, modern materials confer considerable strength and at the same time permit very light weight.

RECORD-BREAKING EVENTS

AIR ACES

Combat in the air personalizes conflict between two nations, with pilots depending very much on their own skill, and that of their crew; in early encounters it was usually possible to see the pilot with whom you were in combat. It is not surprising therefore that, in the First World War especially, the battle for control of the air was seen as a personal fight by its participants, and thus evolved the system of designating individual pilots as aces. In France and the United States five aerial victories were necessary for mention in official communiqués. Germany required ten, but Great Britain did not officially note individual totals.

Major Erich Hartmann, who flew day fighters in the Second World War, has scored more victories in the air than any other pilot, with a total of 352.

At the head of the list for the First World War is the celebrated 'Red Baron' – **Manfred von Richthofen** – with 80, followed by **Capitaine René P. Fonck** of France, with 75, and Britain's **Major E. C. Mannock** with 73.

In the Second World War, German pilots dominated the top of the list because of the special circumstances which existed on the Russian front in 1941/42. The top-scoring pilot of other major combatant nations was accredited with the victories noted in parentheses: Japan (103), Russia (62), America (40), Britain (38).

WOMEN AVIATORS

Traditionally, aviation is regarded as a man's world, but convention should not blind us to the fact that women have accomplished many famous pioneering flights.

Amy Johnson became, in 1930, the first woman to fly solo between London and Australia, in a de Havilland Gipsy Moth; her journey took 19 days.

Amelia Earhart was the first woman to make a solo North Atlantic crossing, in 1932. Three years later she made the first solo flight from Hawaii to California. In 1937 she vanished over the Pacific, while attempting a round-the-world trip.

Jean Batten, from New Zealand, became the first woman to cross the South Atlantic solo, during the period 11–13th November 1935.

Hanna Reitsch, the famous German pilot and confidante of Hitler, was the first woman to fly a helicopter, in 1938.

Jacqueline Cochrane, the celebrated American aviator, learned to fly during her annual holiday in 1932. She achieved a whole string of successes, after gaining her pilot's licence only three weeks from beginning flight training. She trained women pilots in the war; became, in 1953, the first woman to fly faster than the speed of sound and, later, the first to exceed Mach 2; she has also set world jet speed records for 15,100 and 500 kilometres.

Sheila Scott of Britain flew solo around the world, between 18th May and 20th June 1966, to establish a new round-the-world speed record in Class 3. It was also the first round-the-world solo flight by a British pilot.

CIRCLING THE EARTH

Natural obstacles were a challenge that early aviators felt compelled to meet. They presented a danger too, since in case of accident help might be very remote.

These are just a few landmarks in man's conquest of the air.

25th July 1909 Louis Blériot crosses the English Channel.

11th September 1910 first crossing of the Irish Sea.

23rd September 1910 Georges Chavez flies over the Alps.

23rd September 1913 first air crossing of the Mediterranean.

30th July 1914 first crossing of the North Sea by an aeroplane.

13th April 1918 first flight over the Andes.

May 1919 first crossing of the Atlantic (see page 4).

14–15th June 1919 Alcock and Brown make the first non-stop Atlantic journey.

7th August 1919 the Rockies are crossed.

9th May 1926 first flight over the North Pole.

20–21st May 1927 Charles Lindbergh makes the first solo non-stop Atlantic crossing in 'Spirit of St Louis'.

14–15th October 1927 first non-stop crossing of the South Atlantic.

31st May–9th June 1928 first trans-Pacific flight.

28–29th November 1929 first flight over the South Pole.

3rd April 1933 first flight over Everest

15–22nd July 1933 first solo round-the-world trip.

21st July 1969 Neil Armstrong becomes the first man on the moon.

SPEED FEATS
Speed is one way of measuring man's achievements in the air. The following are just a few of the men who have at one time held the world absolute record for speed in the atmosphere.

Paul Tissandier (French), 34.03mph, 1909.

Léon Morane (French), 66.18mph, 1910.

Julés Védrines (French), 108.16mph, 1912.

Lieutenant A. J. Williams (American), 267.16mph, 1923.

Group Captain H. J. Wilson (British), 606.25mph, 1945.

Lieutenant P. Twiss (British), 1,131.76mph, 1956.

Major J. W. Rogers (American), 1,525.93mph, 1959.

Colonel R. L. Stephens (American), 2,070.10mph, 1965.

Captain E. W. Joersz and Major G. T. Morgan Jr. (American), 2,189mph, 1976.

DISTANCE FEATS
The world absolute distance record is another challenge that aviators have always been willing to contest. These are a selection of the record-holders:

A. Santos-Dumont (Brazilian), 772 feet, November 1906.

H. Farman (French), 1.25 miles, March 1908.

L. Delagrange (French), 7.92 miles, May 1908.

L. Delagrange (French), 14.99 miles, September 1908.

Wilbur Wright (American), 62 miles, December 1908.

H. Farman (French), 111.8 miles, August 1909.

Jan Olieslagers (Belgian), 244 miles, July 1910.

J. Fourny (French), 628.1 miles, September 1912.

Captains L. Arrachart and H. Lemaître (French), 1,967 miles, February 1925.

Captain L. Arrachart and Adjutant Arrachart (French), 2,675 miles, June 1926.

R. N. Boardman and J. Polando (American) 5,011 miles, July 1931.

Colonel Irving and Lieutenant-Colonel Stawley (American), 7,916 miles, November 1945.

Commander T. Davis and E. P. Rankin (American), 11,235.6 miles, September 1946.

Major Clyde P. Evely (American), 12,532.3 miles, January 1962.

WORLD WAR II

For the people of Britain, the Supermarine Spitfire has a unique place in the nation's history of the Second World War. It was the only Allied fighter built throughout the war, at the end of which more than 20,000 had been built for the RAF, in over 40 versions. The Spitfire, together with the Hawker Hurricane, was decisive in defeating the Luftwaffe in the Battle of Britain. It served in most theatres of war in a fighter role, as well as for reconnaissance. It was used post-war in the Far and Middle East. Successive versions brought enormous improvements in performance, and by 1945 its power had increased 100 per cent, weight 40 per cent, maximum speed 35 per cent, and rate of climb 80 per cent.

The North American P-51 Mustang fighter (*right*) was one of the most successful aircraft of the Second World War. Manufactured in the United States, it was built initially to RAF requirements, and only later saw service with the USAAF.

The first prototype was built in just over 100 days – a record – and made its maiden flight in October 1940. The first machines reached Britain in October 1941, and were used from 1942 for cross-Channel sweeps and raids on Germany. Later versions were also used to attack flying-bombs.

Shortly before the end of the war, the P-82 Twin Mustang was formed by joining two P-51s together, and these were used for long-range escort duties.

Behind the Mustang on the flight line is a B-25 Mitchell (see page 43).

The Boeing Stearman Kaydet two-seat primary trainer (*bottom*) is one of numerous versions of this useful training craft. Such planes, including an advanced trainer, were produced during the late 1930s and early 1940s by the former Stearman company, which was incorporated into Boeing in 1938. Many were bought by the US Navy and Army, as well as by Cuba, the Philippines, Venezuela and Brazil, among others. The naval versions could be supplied with interchangeable wheel and float landing-gear.

The Model PT-17 had a cruising speed of 96mph, a ceiling of 13,200 feet, and an endurance of 3.9 hours.

The Fairchild PT-19 (*right*) is a two-seat light training monoplane that saw service with the US Air Force during the Second World War. Its endurance was four hours, its cruising speed 120mph, and its ceiling 16,000 feet.
The Lockheed P-38 (*top, opposite*) has RAF markings. Nearly 10,000 examples of this highly successful fighter were built, destroying more enemy aircraft in Pacific campaigns than any other fighter. Over 1000 planes were modified for a reconnaissance role.

The Grumman F6F Hellcat (*bottom, opposite*) was the US Navy's most successful fighter. The plane scored over three-quarters of that service's combat victories during the Second World War. The prototype first flew in 1942, and the plane came into service six months later. By the end of 1945 over 12,000 of this remarkably effective aircraft had been built.

The Fairy Swordfish torpedo bomber (*below*) nicknamed 'the Stringbag', saw service with the Fleet Air Arm throughout the war. A carrier-based plane, it took part in many operations: among them the Norwegian campaign in 1940, the hunt for the *Bismark*, the attack on the Italian fleet at Taranto in 1940, and the unsuccessful attempt to prevent the Channel-dash of the *Scharnhorst*, *Gneisenau* and *Prinz Eugen* in February 1942.
Nearly 2400 were built, and the plane outlasted its intended successors.

The Westland Lysander (*top, opposite*), nicknamed 'Lizzie', was a close-support aircraft built for artillery spotting and reconnaissance. The most famous version was the Lysander III, which was used during the war for dropping and picking up Allied agents in Nazi-occupied Europe, especially in France.

The Grumman Duck (*bottom, opposite*) is one of a series of naval reconnaissance amphibians used during and after the war. Cheap and versatile, it was particularly useful for island-hopping.

Bombers

The Boeing B-17 Flying Fortress, (*below*) was used by the USAAF in bombing raids in practically every theatre, and more than 12,000 were built. In the daylight raids on Germany, the Flying Fortress suffered enormous losses at first, because no fighters then had sufficient range to act as escorts.

The Heinkel He 111 bomber (*opposite*) was licence-built in Spain for the Spanish Air Force. It was first used as a high-speed commercial plane by Lufthansa in 1936, but in the early part of the war it became one of the Luftwaffe's principal bombers. It was used in the attacks on Poland, Denmark and Norway, and on the Royal Navy in the North Sea. It also took part in the Battle of Britain, where it proved to be under-armed and too slow. Its bomb-load, range and altitude were also inadequate for successful strategic operations.

The Avro Lancaster (*right*) was Britain's most
successful four-engine long-range night bomber.
Developed from the unsuccessful twin-engined
Manchester, it came into service in 1942, and
took part in raids on Germany. 31 Lancasters
attacked and sank the German battleship
Tirpitz in November 1944, and 19 specially-
adapted Lancasters from 617 Squadron – the
'Dambusters' – bombed the Mohne and Eder
dams in May 1943.
After the war, the Lancaster was used for a
number of years for reconnaissance.

(*Below*) A Consolidated B-24 Liberator bomber
with its crew. Over 18,000 Liberators were
built – more than any other American plane.
They were used also for reconnaissance and
transport by the Allied air forces, and after the
war many British prisoners of war were flown
home in them.

The North American B-25 Mitchell medium-
range bomber (*below right*), named after Colonel
William Mitchell, was one of the most out-
standing bombers used by American forces
during the Second World War.

MODERN
AIR FORCES

The post-war years saw enormous changes in military aircraft of all kinds. Designers and engineers soon went far beyond the knowledge and experience gained during war and, as a result, craft capable of supersonic speeds and armed with sophisticated weapons sytems are now the order of the day in air forces all over the world. The production line of the Dassault-Mirage F-1 (*opposite*) indicates the massive technological involvement as well as the demand, for such ever-developing and expensive equipment.

The Lockheed F-104 Starfighter (*above* and *right*) was the world's first operational fighter capable of sustained speeds above Mach 2. It was originally designed as a high-performance day fighter. The first production model flew in 1956, and it began to come into service two years later. Numerous versions have been built, but by far the most successful is the F-104G, which first flew in 1960, and has been supplied to air forces all over the world. It is now regarded as a multi-role plane, being equipped with a 20mm Vulcan gun, and able to carry up to 4000lb of bombs, or Sidewinder missiles. The F-104G has a ferry range of 1875 miles and a maximum level speed of Mach 2.2. It has also been test-launched with a large booster rocket. Nicknamed, for obvious reasons, 'the missile with a man in it', the Starfighter is also known, less happily, as 'widowmaker', since a number of those which were supplied to the German air force crashed.

The BAC (formerly English Electric) Lightning
(*below* and *right*), the first RAF single-seat
fighter to exceed the speed of sound in level
flight, was also the first true British supersonic
fighter. For the RAF, the Lightning offered
considerable advantages. Its advanced design
made it twice as fast as the fighters that had
preceded it in service; it could also fly higher,
and it boasted a fully-integrated weapons
system.

The prototype F.1 Lightning first flew in 1954,
and in 1958 it became the first British aircraft to
attain Mach 2. The first F.1 production aircraft
flew less than a year later. The F.3 came into
service in 1964, and the F.6 appeared two years
later. This had longer patrol time, longer
supersonic endurance, and could be refuelled
during flight.

By 1974 the Phantom was beginning to replace
the Lightning, but top squadrons are due to
remain in service until the 1980s.

The Grumman F-14A Tomcat (*left* and *above*), one of the most advanced fighters currently in production, was developed for the US Navy. The Tomcat came into service in October 1972, but the first prototype flew in December 1970. A two-seat, variable-geometry, multi-role fighter, it has been described as the US Navy's most lethal carrier-based aircraft.

The three most important functions of the Tomcat are to protect a strike force and clear airspace of enemy fighters; to defend carrier task forces; and to carry out secondary attacks on ground targets. It can attack up to six airborne targets at the same time with Phoenix missiles, and can also carry Sparrow or Sidewinder missiles.

The sweep of the outer wings is adjusted to optimum position automatically during the flight by a Mach sweep programmer, though the pilot can override this.

The Tomcat has a maximum design speed of Mach 2.4, and a ceiling of 50,000 feet.

The Saab Viggen (*above*) a single-seat, all-weather multi-purpose plane, is used as a long-range fighter, and for reconnaissance and attack. Since it came into service with the Swedish air force in 1971 more than 140 have been built.

(*Top, opposite*) A Tupolev Tu-95 (often referred to as Tu-20) is being intercepted by a BAC Lightning (see page 49). The Tu-95, known to NATO as the 'Bear', was the USSR's first intercontinental strategic bomber. Four turboprop engines give a maximum speed of 500mph. It is now used for maritime reconnaissance, and to provide missile guidance information.

(*Bottom, opposite*) is a group of Northrop T-38 Talons. These two-seat basic trainers were the first able to fly at supersonic speed.

The Lockheed U-2 (*overleaf, top left*), a single-seat strategic reconnaissance plane, was designed in the mid-1950s to carry out photographic reconnaissance from what was considered an undetectable height.

The Rockwell OV-10 Bronco (*overleaf, bottom left*) developed originally for the US Marine Corps as a light-armed reconnaissance aircraft suitable for counter-insurgency missions.

The Hawker Siddeley Buccaneer (*overleaf, top right*) is a two-seat, strike and reconnaissance aircraft developed in the late 1950s and used by both the Royal Navy and the RAF.

The Hawker Siddeley Nimrod (*overleaf, bottom right*) is based on the civilian Comet 4. Its main use is for anti-submarine warfare, surveillance and anti-shipping strikes.

COMMERCIAL AIRCRAFT

The vast strides made by commercial airlines in the past 25 years have revolutionized attitudes to travel, and to the size of the world. Of these developments, the Boeing 747 (*left*), the world's largest civil aircraft, is probably the most significant. It carries more passengers than any other plane, thus helping to reduce the actual number of flights, and thereby both fares and noise-levels.

The Vickers Viscount (*left*) evolved as a result of the activities of the Brabazon Committee. Established in December 1942, the task of this committee was to make recommendations to Britain's aircraft industry regarding the development of post-war transport aircraft. The prototype Viscount V630, powered by four of the then-new turboprop engines, flew first in July 1948. In 1950 the Viscount made the first scheduled service flown by a turbine-powered airliner.

The de Havilland Comet 4 (*bottom left*) was evolved from the world's first jet passenger service on 2nd May 1952. The subsequent loss of three Comet 4s as a result of fatigue failure of the cabin structure was a bitter blow to Britain's aircraft industry, for by the time that the failure had been diagnosed and the improved Comet 4 was in service, Boeing in America had jumped into the lead with the larger capacity Model 707.

Boeing's Model 747 'Jumbo jet' was the first of the wide bodied civil transport aircraft which have revolutionized air travel. Lockheed and McDonnell Douglas in America have both produced wide-bodied transports, the Lockheed L-1011 TriStar and the McDonnell Douglas DC-10 (*bottom right*). More than 300 of these latter aircraft had been ordered in late 1978, and the 200 aircraft in service had carried over 170 million passengers by the end of that year.

Concorde

The Concorde (*below* and *right*) produced jointly by the British Aircraft Corporation and the French company, Aérospatiale, was the first supersonic commercial transport aircraft to operate regular scheduled passenger services. The first passenger services were flown simultaneously by Air France and British Airways on 21st January 1976. By mid-1978 the 11 aircraft in service had flown 10,000 hours.

The Russian Tupolev Tu-144 (*bottom*) was nicknamed Concordski in the West. The prototype Tu-144, which first flew on 31st December 1968, was the world's first supersonic transport aircraft to fly. They later became the first commercial transports to exceed Mach 2.

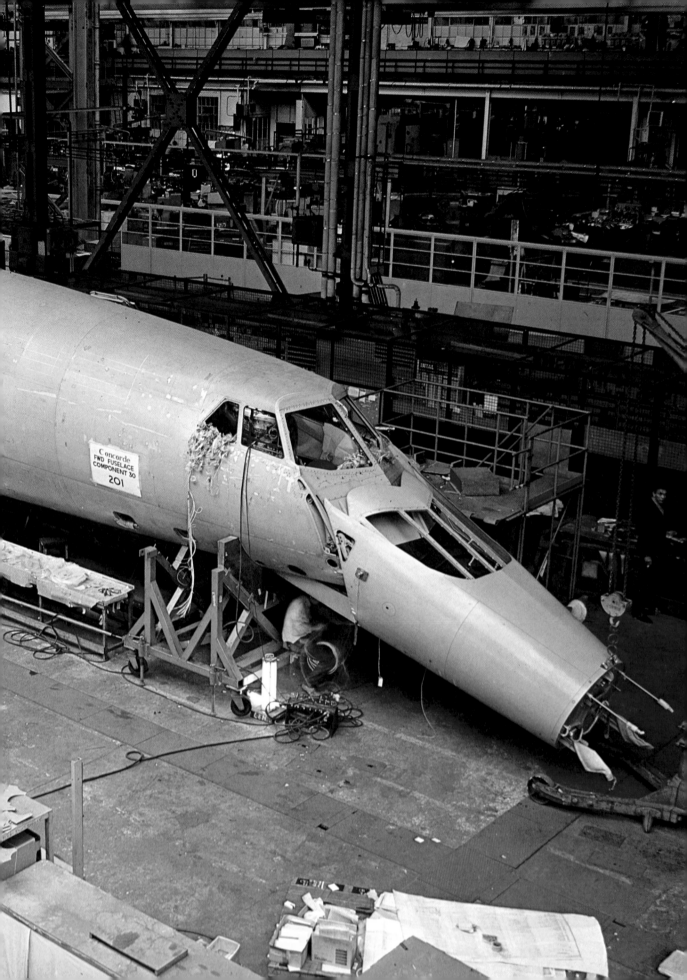

The Boeing 747 'Jumbo jet' (*below*, see also page 59) was announced in 1966, and first flew in 1969. It came into service in the following year, and by the summer of 1978, 407 had been ordered.

The 747 can seat between 385 and 500 passengers. The 747SP, which seats between 288 and 360, is a very long-range version intended for routes with a lower passenger density. It first flew in 1975, and in 1976 it set the world record for a non-stop flight by a commercial aircraft, covering the 10,290 miles between Washington State and Cape Town in 17 hours 22 minutes.

(*Right* and *opposite*) The cockpit and exterior of the Lockheed L1011 TriStar, a short- and medium-range, wide-bodied jet, powered by Rolls-Royce RB211 turbofan engines. It first flew in November 1970.

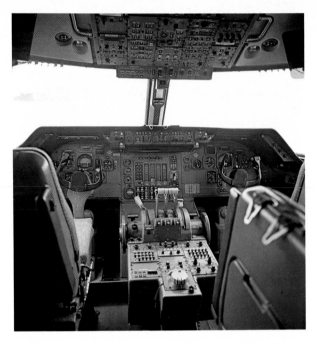

INDEX

This edition published in 1980 by
Octopus Books Limited
59 Grosvenor Street, London W1

ISBN 0 7064 1106 4

© 1979 Octopus Books Limited

Produced by
Mandarin Publishers Limited
22a Westlands Road
Quarry Bay, Hong Kong

Printed in Hong Kong

PDO 79-478